THE TRAIL OF

TURNER

IN NORTH AND SOUTH WALES

Peter Humphries

CONTENTS

J. M. W. Turner, Dolbadern Castle, North Wales, *1800, oil on canvas: 1195 x 902mm. Royal Academy of Arts, London.*

TURNER AND WALES

INTRODUCTION

Joseph Mallord William Turner (1775–1851) was an artist of extraordinary gifts who today enjoys a unique place in British affection. So great has his impact been on our national heritage, that it has been said of him: 'what Shakespeare is in the realm of British literature, Turner is in the realm of art' [1]. He grew to maturity and received his artistic training during the latter part of the eighteenth century — that period which saw the emergence of landscape painting in Britain — and he is generally acclaimed as Britain's greatest landscape painter. Indeed, the writer, John Ruskin (1819–1900), went still further, calling him 'the only perfect landscape painter whom the world has ever seen' [2]. No other contender for that accolade has ever been able to rival Turner's inventive technical complexity, his supreme mastery of atmosphere and his wonderfully subtle and expressive portrayal of light. Those skills were attained and honed gradually during the first ten years of his career, firstly through formal training and meticulous study of his subject matter, then by analysing and emulating the work of other artists, and then increasingly through experimentation and the use of his own fertile imagination. Yet it is interesting to reflect that Turner's progress in those early years was much furthered, and his working methods partly moulded, by his experiences of the volatile weather and widely varying landscapes of Wales — its mountains, its rivers and coasts, as well as the evocative ruins of its chequered past.

As a young artist, on the threshold of his career, he undertook five sketching and painting tours in Wales, between 1792 and 1799, thus establishing the pattern of travelling and meticulous recording of detail in his sketchbooks that he was to maintain throughout his life. Andrew Wilton described these early Welsh pictures of Turner's as 'works of a richness and vitality, a readiness of inspiration and a fecundity of technical invention, that rival those of any other period of his life, and [which] must count among the most intense of all romantic landscapes' [3]. Turner was to return to Wales only once more in his life, very briefly in 1808, and yet, much later in his career, when his artistic style had evolved and matured, he was to draw again on subjects from those early Welsh tours in his series of watercolours entitled *Picturesque Views of England and Wales*, completed between 1825 and 1836. Examples of his work from all of these periods are reproduced in this booklet as we follow his progress in Wales and chart the visual record that he made of ruined buildings now in the care of Cadw and others.

J. M. W. Turner, Self-portrait, *about 1798, oil on canvas: 745 x 585mm. Turner Bequest, Tate Gallery, London (458).*

EARLY LIFE

Turner came from relatively humble origins in a poor part of central London. Perhaps it was this lowly background that made him uneasy as he grew in artistic stature, perhaps it was a trait he inherited, but whatever the reason he seems always to have remained obsessively secretive about his upbringing and his private life, just as he was about his art. A contemporary once remarked that '... his life partook of the character of his works; it was mysterious and nothing seemed to please him so much as to try and puzzle you'[4]. When he was born, in 1775, his father had rented premises in Maiden Lane, off London's Covent Garden, where he carried on business as a barber and wig maker. His mother, several years older than her husband, was evidently possessed of a volatile disposition and prone to violent outbursts; her uneven mental state gradually worsened over the years, and she was ultimately confined to Bethlem Hospital for the insane, where she died in 1804.

The young Turner was brought up in a small house adjoining the barber's shop and, like many people who later achieve greatness, he seems to have shown a very early aptitude for his craft. His father evidently encouraged the boy's developing passion for art and proudly exhibited his drawings for sale in the window of his shop. During these early years, no doubt because of the increasing difficulties at home, William spent extended periods staying with family friends and relatives in various parts of the country. There he would eagerly seek out new locations to practise his developing skills in drawing — indeed, so single-minded was he in this endeavour that he more than once incurred the displeasure of his hosts, who sometimes thought him surly and ill-mannered.

These sojourns seem to have begun from the age of about ten, when he was sent to stay with his uncle in the more rural surroundings of New Brentford, Middlesex. It is from this time that we have the earliest probable evidence of his undertakings in the form of a series of around seventy topographical etchings for the colouring of which he was apparently paid two-pence a plate[5]. The earliest signed and dated drawings come from a year or two later, and within a further two years he had found employment as a draughtsman in the offices of various architects. One of these, so a story goes, upbraided him for colouring in naturalistic reflections on the windows in an architectural perspective drawing and insisted that he repaint them the conventional uniform dark grey. 'It will spoil my drawing,' complained young William. 'Rather that than my work' came the determined reply — though apparently the architect later adopted the same practice himself after Turner had left his employ[6]. By the end of that year, 1789, when William was still only fourteen, he had progressed from working in architects' offices to the studio of one of the country's leading topographical draughtsmen, Thomas Malton (1726–1801), 'my real master', as he was later to describe him[7]. That year, too, after his talents had caught the attention of one of his barber-father's customers with connections in the art world, he was put forward for and admitted a member of the Royal Academy Schools, then based in Somerset House[8], where he was to continue with his artistic training over the course of the next few years. The following year, 1790, he made a significant achievement for one so young, by having a watercolour included in a Royal Academy exhibition. It was to be the beginning of an almost unbroken series of annual showings at the Academy over a period of sixty years, and this was very soon to become his spiritual home.

JOURNEYS INTO SOUTH WALES

In 1791 Turner went to stay with friends of his father in Bristol, the Narraways. He spent so much of the time scrambling about the Avon Gorge in search of viewpoints from which to draw, that they nicknamed him 'The Prince of The Rocks'[9], but it was also then that he evidently made his first acquaintance with Wales, crossing by the ferry to Beachley and drawing the tiny ruined island chapel at the mouth of the Wye[10]. The summer of the following year, when he was just seventeen, he stayed with the Narraways again, this time using the visit as a springboard for his first artistic foray into Wales. Crossing once more by the ferry, he made his way up the Wye valley via Chepstow Castle and Tintern Abbey to Monmouth, thence to Abergavenny and northwards to the priory of Llanthony in the Black Mountains, before following the course of the Wye up to Rhayader and on to Devil's Bridge, then finally returning to London via Hereford and Oxford[11]. After the west country, this was the first extended sketching tour the young Turner had undertaken, though, oddly, few pencil drawings have survived from it. Nevertheless, several finished watercolours of buildings and scenery seen on that visit were completed over the following winter and subsequently (pp. 14, 16, 18).

In 1794 he made a second journey into Wales, although this time he seems to have done so as a brief extension to an antiquarian tour of the English Midlands — a commission received from a publisher to produce views suitable for engraving. These diversions seem to have taken him as far as Flint, on the Dee estuary, and then southwards by way of Wrexham to Llangollen and the abbey of Valle Crucis at the foot of the Horseshoe Pass. His fully worked up watercolour of the abbey (p. 36) was completed soon after that tour.

Giovanni Battista Piranesi, The So-Called Villa of Maecenas at Tivoli. Interior, *1764, engraving: 470 x 620mm (Hind 73). Turner was introduced to Piranesi's prints by Sir Richard Colt Hoare in 1795, and their lighting effects and sense of scale were soon to manifest themselves in his own work — compare with his watercolour of Ewenny (p. 21).*

The following year, 1795, saw Turner's first detailed tour of the southern part of Wales. This time he made rather more careful preparations, working out his itinerary in advance with notes on the principal points of interest, and taking with him two sketchbooks of differing sizes — one for pencil sketches and notes, the other to use for more detailed drawings. Setting out again from Bristol, he followed the main south Wales coast road through Newport and Cardiff, then into the Vale of Glamorgan to Ewenny Priory and on westwards through Margam, Neath and Swansea to visit the castles of Kidwelly, Llansteffan and Laugharne; thence into Pembrokeshire, where his travels took him through to the farthest point at St Davids, before returning by way of the Tywi and Usk valleys. By this time his sketches were beginning to attract the interest of a number of wealthy patrons — indeed, such was his industry and his business acumen that he was rarely ever to be short of commissions throughout his long career. One of his more influential patrons at this period was Sir Richard Colt Hoare (1758–1838) of Stourhead, Wiltshire, whose house he visited later in 1795 and whose collection included a painting by Rembrandt (1607–69), prints by Piranesi (1720–78), and large Italian views by the innovative Swiss watercolourist Abraham-Louis-Rodolphe Ducros (1748–1810), all of which were to have a profound effect on the young artist.

That 1795 tour resulted in a considerable number of finished works over the course of the next few years,

J. M. W. Turner, Fishermen at Sea *('The Cholmeley Sea Piece'), 1796, oil on canvas: 915 x 1224mm. Tate Gallery, London (1585). This fine nocturnal study was Turner's first oil painting to be exhibited and was shown at the Royal Academy that year.*

perhaps the finest of which was the splendid watercolour of the *Trancept of Ewenny Priory, Glamorganshire* (p. 21) exhibited in 1797. With its wonderfully evocative contrast of sunlight and shadow piercing the gloom of the Romanesque interior, this clearly betrays the influence of both Piranesi and Rembrandt. Other subjects to emerge from that period were coloured, but unfinished sketches of Llansteffan Castle (p. 27) and the Bishop's Palace at St Davids (p. 34), as well as fully finished watercolours of Newport Castle (p. 20), and also — his other *tour de force* from that 1795 trip — *Llandilo Bridge and Dinevor Castle* (p. 24). This was another subtle and beautifully lit study in evening light with its ancient hilltop castle, collapsed stone bridge and women washing their clothes in the river by an uprooted tree (recent evidence has come to light that Turner experimented with an unusual technique in his execution of this picture [12] — see p. 25).

Thus far, practically all of Turner's output had been in watercolour — a medium that had found growing favour among serious artists in the eighteenth century because it was quicker and easier to use than oil and it dried rapidly. However, the following year, 1796, in addition to several important watercolours, he exhibited his first oil painting at the Royal Academy, a luminous moonlit seascape entitled *Fishermen at Sea*. In it, as in a number of his pictures from this early period, can be seen the stylistic influence of his older contemporary, an established member of the Royal Academy, Philippe Jacques de Loutherbourg (1740–1812). But although watercolour was to remain important to Turner throughout his life, his technical development in the medium was profoundly affected by his increasing experience with oil — just as his watercolour work was later to be reflected in his oil technique. Despite Turner's enormous outpouring of watercolour subjects, most of the pictures for which he is best known are oil paintings. Oil was considered a more 'serious' medium. This was a factor which he had to come to terms with early in his career for at that time it was only possible to gain membership of the Royal Academy — a status he dearly wanted — by exhibiting oil paintings.

WIDER EXPLORATION

In the summer of 1798 Turner embarked on a further tour of Wales; this time it was to be his most ambitious journey yet, for he planned to visit virtually the whole of the country, and he took with him at least five sketchbooks in which to record his impressions. Although he did not apparently work out a detailed itinerary in advance, he did make a long list of places worth visiting, most of which were castles. With his early training in architectural drawing to support him, Turner was following the well-trodden path of preceding generations of itinerant antiquarian topographers like the Buck brothers, Paul Sandby (1725–1809) and Thomas Pennant (1726–98). The latter part of the eighteenth century, it should be remembered, was dominated by the artistic fashion for the 'Picturesque' — a preoccupation with the pictorial values of architecture and landscape in combination. What constituted 'Picturesqueness' was the subject of much academic debate, but it was chiefly characterized by pleasing variety, irregularity, asymmetry, and interesting textures. Medieval ruins in a natural landscape were thus quintessentially Picturesque, and artists toured the country in search of such views which they could depict and place before an eager public. Increasingly, however, Turner used historic sites to impart a moral dimension to his pictures, to show the transience, or destructiveness of human endeavour and its feebleness in the face of natural elements — such ruins helped him to convey 'all the littleness of man', as he was later to express it [13]. As previously, the visit began with a stay in Bristol at his friends the Narraways. This time the twenty-three-year-old Turner succeeded in thoroughly vexing his hosts by his thoughtless conduct. Mr Narraway's niece, Ann Dart, later recalled in correspondence to John Ruskin the 'plain uninteresting youth both in manners and appearance ... [who] would talk of nothing but his drawings, and of the places he should go for sketching.' She recollected with some disdain that 'Turner went from my uncle's house on a sketching tour in North Wales. My uncle gave him a pony, and lent him a saddle, bridle and cloak, but these he never returned. My uncle used to exclaim what an ungrateful little scoundrel ...' [14]. This time Turner again explored the valleys of the Wye and Usk, before turning down the south Wales valley of the Taff to Cardiff and travelling westwards by way of the Tywi valley to Cardigan. From there his route took him north through Aberystwyth and all around Snowdonia, then along the north Wales coast and back down the border to Hereford.

The five surviving sketchbooks from that 1798 tour provide a vivid insight into the working methods that Turner was developing at that time [15]. The larger books are filled with careful and elaborate pencil drawings, often partly or fully washed in watercolour, while the smaller ones are a jumble of rapid notes, sometimes using abbreviations to denote colours or weather conditions, and quick pencil sketches of details or viewpoints for potential future use. In order to capture the immensely varied and overwhelming scenery of the country he was travelling through, he was obliged to devise his own method of visual shorthand to convey what he felt to be the complete experience of the view before him. This on-site technique, which he developed in Wales, was to stay with him for the remainder of his life. His aim was to make as full a record as possible to take away and use later to supplement his acute and retentive visual memory. Throughout his life he was to remain an assiduous collector and recorder of minute detail; everything went into his sketchbooks to be reordered and reused at will, either in a finished work shortly after a tour, or at some much later time. This constantly growing private reference library was invaluable to him — Turner made more than fifty-six tours throughout Britain and the Continent during his long career [16] — and it formed a large part of the vast collection, now known as the *Turner Bequest*, which came to the nation after his death in 1851. In this, his sketchbooks alone numbered around 300, and the whole collection amounted to more than 30,000 assorted pencil sketches, rough colour studies and finished pictures — eloquent testimony to the artist's phenomenal industry and his insatiable visual curiosity.

Two fully-coloured studies from sketchbooks he took with him on that tour of 1798 are reproduced here: a view of Carreg Cennen (p. 23) from the *Dynevor Castle* sketchbook and, from the much larger *Hereford Court* sketchbook, one of Cilgerran Castle (p. 35). One other picture resulting from the tour, but completed early in 1799 and exhibited at the Royal Academy that year, is also shown here: it is an oil painting entitled *Harlech Castle, from Twgwyn ferry, summer's evening twilight* (inside back cover). The deep tones and gentle golden sky betray the influence of Richard Wilson (1714–82), the Welsh landscape painter of the preceding generation whose style had become an important model for Turner at this time. Through Wilson, however, the influence extends back even further to the great seventeenth-century French landscape artist, Claude Lorrain (1600–82), who had become Wilson's own model and whose work was to act as a major influence on Turner from this time onwards — for in Claude 'Turner perceived a completely harmonious expression of a physically ideal world that for him clearly set the standard of beauty to which all landscape painting should aspire' [17]. But although it was, and still is, common for artists to model their style on that of some earlier master, it was not easy in Turner's day to gain access to such works; virtually all were in private ownership for there were no public collections in Britain before 1814. Almost the sole available means of studying pictures was through the secondary medium of prints. Turner thus began steadily to familiarize himself with the work of Claude and other great masters such as Poussin (1594–1665), Rembrandt, Rosa (1615–73) and Titian (1489–1576), but as his travels took him ever further afield and his network of wealthy patrons grew he would grasp every opportunity to see the originals for himself. It was to become a continual process which both broadened his aspirations and helped fuel his own fertile imagination.

EXPLORING NEW HORIZONS

One other clear source of inspiration to the developing Turner at this period was the majestic mountain scenery of Snowdonia he had experienced in 1798, and he was drawn back to the area again for a final visit the following year whilst returning from a commission in Lancashire. This time, as well as his sketchbooks, he took with him some larger sheets of drawing paper to enable him to record more fully his impressions of the vast mountain scenery around Snowdon. He set off imbued with an acute sense of history, inspired not only by the ringing prose of Thomas Pennant's *Tour in Wales*, but by his own emerging ambitions to combine landscape painting with history and poetry, as well as by the towering presence of the mountains themselves. The paintings that he produced around these closing years of the eighteenth century were amongst the most significant of his whole career. By now he had completed his formal schooling and was gradually gaining in confidence and experience. His work at this time underwent something of a transformation and he now began to invest his pictures with additional layers of meaning, taking them far beyond mere depictions of topography. This diversification included some of his earliest attempts in the genre of 'History' painting, then regarded as the highest form of art, where classical, biblical and other historical themes were developed into pictorial subjects. It also comprised a number of essays in the fashionable art of the 'Sublime', which exploited the reactions of fear and astonishment to provoke a more profound emotional response; here the works of nature were presented unadorned, and the pictures are characterized by dark, mysterious mountain landscapes of awe-inspiring scale and grandeur. Taking advantage, too, of the Royal Academy's new ruling of 1798 allowing the use of supportive text alongside picture titles, Turner began to augment and interpret the impact of his paintings with lengthy titles and with additional lines of poetry. In his day it was a readily accepted view that poetry and painting were collaborative, or 'sister arts' — 'Poesy & Painting, being sisters, agree entirely ... We cannot make good Painters without some aid from Poesy' was how he himself was to rationalize it in a lecture to the Royal Academy some years afterwards [18]. Throughout his life Turner was an avid and eclectic reader, and he had become thoroughly immersed in poetry even at this early stage in his career.

His earliest Welsh attempts in this vein were exhibited at the Academy in 1799 and are very much in the manner of Claude. One was *Harlech Castle, from Twgwyn ferry, summer's evening twilight* (inside back cover); it was accompanied by lines from Book IV of Milton's *Paradise Lost* which amplify and reinforce the strong pictorial imagery of the painting. In another sunset subject, his watercolour *Caernarvon Castle* (inside front cover), Turner achieved a radiance of effect so like an oil painting that one visitor to the Academy exhibition that year was driven to remark that it had a 'depth and force of tone, which I had never before conceived attainable with such untoward implements'[19]. The picture was accompanied by these lines from Canto 1 of Mallet's *Amyntor and Theodora* intended to echo the splendidly rendered effect of the sun's rays — one of a number of instances where the artist chose quotations reflecting his own lifelong preoccupation with the effects of light:

> *Now rose*
> *Sweet Evening, solemn hour, the sun declin'd,*
> *Hung golden o'er this nether firmament,*
> *Whose broad cerulean mirror, calmly bright,*
> *Gave back his beamy visage to the sky*
> *With splendour undiminish'd.*

1799 was also the year in which the twenty-four-year-old Turner put himself forward the second time (after having been unsuccessful the previous year) for election as Associate of the Royal Academy. So keen was he to gain full acceptance from that august institution to which, by now, he owed most of his formal tuition that he went to great lengths to court favour in Academy circles. One regular confidant was the Academician Joseph Farington (1747–1821), to whom he happily divulged some of his own working methods — this in complete contrast to the obsessive secrecy with which he was to surround himself and his work in later life. Later that year, after one such visit, Farington noted that the artist avoided the slavish

Claude Lorrain, Seaport with Embarkation of the Queen of Sheba, *1648, oil on canvas: 1491 x 1967mm. National Gallery, London (NG14). This painting was very influential on Turner's art — compare with* Caernarvon Castle *(inside front cover); it belonged to John Julius Angerstein, who later presented his collection to the nation as the nucleus of the National Gallery.*

adoption of any particular style of painting because 'He thinks it can produce nothing but manner and sameness ... Turner has no settled process but drives the colours abt. till he has expressed the idea in his mind'[20]. In the event Turner need not have worried: this time his election as Associate went through without a hitch; the next step was full membership.

THE ASPIRING ACADEMICIAN

Following his last Welsh tour of that year and his renewed experience of Snowdonia, Turner was to produce a substantial outpouring of mountain scenes, whose sombre tones and sense of looming mystery fully embraced conventional definitions of the 'Sublime'. Two other Welsh castle pictures of the period 1799–1800 are particularly worthy of note: his watercolour *Caernarvon Castle, North Wales* (below) and the oil *Dolbadern Castle, North Wales* (p. 2). Both of these are historical subjects, and in each, although their titles give no hint of it, the artist has progressed a stage beyond his previous endeavours with the associative use of verse. Here, instead of using poetic metaphor to supply the missing visual components of his pictures, he uses poetry as a supplementary narrative to explain the visual clues that he now weaves into the pictures themselves[21]. The *Caernarvon* is a distant view of the castle set amidst a pastoral landscape at evening time; in the foreground a small group of figures sits before a bard who plays his

J.M.W. Turner, Caernarvon Castle, North Wales, *1799–1800, pencil and watercolour with scratching-out and stopping-out: 663 x 994mm. Tate Gallery, London, Turner Bequest (TB LXXX-M).*

harp whilst pointing toward the castle. Turner could doubtless expect the discerning viewers of his own day — unlike modern art audiences — to be acquainted with the fate of the oft-illustrated hero in Thomas Gray's poem *The Bard* and to recognize him in this painting. The whole scene is a powerful allusion to the subjection of the Welsh by King Edward I (1272–1307), though a contemporary reference to the expansionist ambitions of Napoleon (1769–1821) was doubtless intended too, and it was accompanied in the Academy catalogue by these lines of verse which have since been attributed to Turner himself:

And now on Arvon's haughty tow'rs
The Bard the song of pity pours,
For oft on Mona's distant hills he sighs,
Where jealous of the minstrel band,
The tyrant drench'd with blood the land,
And charm'd with horror, triumph'd in their cries,
The swains of Arvon round him throng,
And join the sorrows of his song.

Another large uncompleted watercolour of this period was apparently intended to form a pair to this picture[22]. Entitled *Scene in the Welsh mountains with an army on the march*, it was probably planned, like the *Caernarfon*, to illustrate Gray's ode, and is one of a group of works with a bardic theme by Turner at this time, although here the central figure of the bard is missing.

The *Dolbadern* is a somewhat larger view in oils, based upon sketches the artist had made in the Llanberis Pass in 1798 and 1799. With its upright composition of dark, brooding mountains and the solitary castle tower high above, emerging through a bright halo of sunlight, this is very much an exercise in the 'Sublime'. Far below, and deliberately placed immediately beneath the castle, are four figures: two soldiers standing guard over a kneeling prisoner, his wrists bound behind him, whilst another figure points upwards toward the castle[23]. Accompanying the picture title in the Royal Academy catalogue were these lines which may also be Turner's own:

How awful is the silence of the waste,
Where nature lifts her mountains to the sky,
Majestic solitude, behold the tower
Where hopeless OWEN, long imprison'd, pined
And wrung his hands for liberty, in vain.

The 'Owen' of the poem is Owain Goch, imprisoned between 1255 and 1277 by his powerful younger brother Llywelyn the Last (d. 1282), prince of Gwynedd, after a political family feud. According to the sixteenth-century historian, John Leland, that imprisonment took place in Dolbadarn Castle. Owain was eventually freed under the settlement imposed by Edward I at the Treaty of Aberconwy in 1277. The kneeling prisoner depicted in the painting, placed so significantly directly beneath the looming castle tower, is presumably he. Turner evidently spent some time in working out the composition of this view, making a number of preliminary sketches for it, and it demonstrates well a trait that became commonplace in his pictures from about this time onwards: an economy with topographical truth. The multiplicity of hurried sketches, details and partly, or fully worked-up views that Turner had been amassing in his sketchbooks were his way of gaining a full and comprehensive understanding of a particular view. But they also enabled him later to rearrange, or even merge certain features and viewpoints in order to adjust and improve the composition of his picture — 'to select, combine and concentrate that which is beautiful in nature and admirable in art is ... the business of the landscape painter' was how he summarized his philosophy in a lecture to the Academy some years later. Here, as became abundantly clear when the photographers for this booklet were trying to match this view of Turner's (p. 44), he has almost completely ignored reality for it is impossible to obtain such a view; the castle tower has been heightened, the mountains raised and the whole valley narrowed. Be all of that as it may, the composition does make an undeniably powerful image. By this time Turner owed a great debt to his five sketching tours in Wales, for the varied landscapes he had encountered there had certainly helped him to find his own individual voice as a painter. It was a fact that he himself recognized. When, on 12 February 1802, he was elected to the coveted status of full Academician, it was entirely appropriate that this, perhaps his most carefully planned picture to date, was the painting that he offered as his Diploma piece.

Yet despite Turner's undoubted propensity for making sometimes major adjustments to the natural topography in order to create mood or atmosphere, it is interesting to note that he remained generally faithful to the architectural details of the buildings he depicted — though he frequently exaggerated details for the sake of effect. A great many pictures from the first decade of his career in the 1790s are fine architectural studies in their own right. The two views of Tintern Abbey (pp. 16–17) and the interior of Ewenny Priory (p. 21) illustrate the point here and the impression will be reinforced by a glance through Wilton's catalogue of the artist's watercolour work[24]. Although, in later life, buildings featured much less prominently in Turner's art, his concern for architectural accuracy remained.

After 1799 Turner made no more extended visits into Wales. By that time he seems to have drawn what he could from the history and topography of the country, and was ready to move his career forward elsewhere. Thus far he had confined his travels to England and Wales. The wars with France, which had convulsed so much of Europe from 1793 onwards, had put an abrupt end to the aristocratic and the aesthetic grand tour alike. Artists in search of the 'Picturesque' and 'Sublime' turned to the wilder landscape of Wales and Scotland, where the gradual expansion of turnpikes and coach services was beginning to open up greater possibilities of travel. In 1801 Turner made an extensive tour of Scotland, but the following year, taking advantage of a respite in European hostilities resulting from the Treaty of Amiens, he was able to make his first crossing to the Continent, including a wide-ranging excursion in the Alps. Both these tours provided him with further opportunities to extend his artistic command of the 'Sublime', which was to continue as an abiding theme throughout his career. But in addition to depicting the majesty of the natural world — whether in the form of dramatic scenery, or the unpredictable forces of weather or of water — it was the relationship between nature and humanity that increasingly absorbed Turner's interest. From early in his career his pictures had often included local human colour in the foreground, following eighteenth-century topographical convention. In 1794 there was the girl tending pigs before Valle Crucis Abbey (p. 36), in 1796 the countrywomen washing their clothes in the river by Llandeilo bridge (p. 24), and the woman feeding chickens in the vaulted crossing of Ewenny Priory (p. 21) exhibited the following year. Now, as he matured, his vision widened to embrace all aspects of human nature and activity in the world as he knew it.

ENGLAND AND WALES

In the following decades Turner embarked on a number of grand projects in which he set out to depict the diverse life and landscape of the nation. Comprising watercolour views in series, all were produced specifically for the medium of engraving, which would allow them to be seen by a very much wider audience. It was a concept that derived from the common eighteenth-century practice of publishing sets of engraved picturesque views. Between 1810 and 1838 Turner produced no less than eleven series, comprising over 250 views. Of all these projects, the most ambitious in scope and in execution — and the last that concerns us in the context of this booklet — was *Picturesque Views in England and Wales*. Effectively Turner's final published series, this ran from 1825 right through to 1838 and it was, in Andrew Wilton's words, '... the central document of his art, and the most complete expression of a profound theme in the history of landscape'[25].

Picturesque Views in England and Wales was the fruit of a collaboration between Turner and the engraver and publisher Charles Heath (1785–1848). The two men had known each other and worked successfully together for many years, and Heath, writing to a banker friend in 1825, expressed the view that this new project would 'be the best and most lucrative speculation ever executed of that description'[26]. There were to be 120 watercolours in all, transferred onto copper plates by a number of top-class engravers working under Heath's and Turner's direct supervision. But for all its ambitions, and despite the enthusiasm with which both men embarked upon it, the project was dogged by misfortune almost from the outset. Engraving onto metal was a tedious and exacting process, with the unfortunate engraver working up to fourteen hours a day for anything up to two years to produce a single plate. Thus the first print did not appear until March 1827; and then there was a further setback when the publishers went bankrupt. Heath was unable to find another firm as willing to put up all the capital and, in an attempt to bridge the shortfall himself, his own finances became over-extended. Nevertheless, prints did begin to appear about three times a year from 1827 — four engravings to a set, at prices ranging from fourteen shillings up to a guinea and a half[27] — and their publication carried on for more than ten years. But despite a number of exhibitions aimed at encouraging subscription, the prints failed to sell in sufficient numbers to keep the enterprise financially viable and the scheme ultimately failed. This was due in part to Turner's insistence on using copper plates, rather than the harder alternative of steel (copper gave greater subtlety and refinement of line but, being soft, it dulled quickly with repeated printing, whereas steel allowed many more impressions to be taken from the plate, thereby reducing costs); but it may have been partly because the fashion for topographical engravings was waning. By 1836, when his work on the project finally ceased, Turner had completed only about a hundred watercolours, of which ninety-six were eventually engraved.

The project ruined Charles Heath, and he was forced to sell his own proof set of the engravings in an attempt to offset some of his losses. The publishers, too, endeavoured to recoup by selling off their entire holding. For Turner himself the outcome was a bitter blow; in order to prevent the remaining stock being sold at a knock-down price and so devaluing the whole collection he bought up the lot, copper plates and prints, for the sum of £3,000. This was his final attempt at producing engravings in sets; there was to be no further venture. The financial failure of the project, however, in no way reflects on the quality of the watercolours themselves. During the 1820s and '30s Turner was at the very height of his mature creative powers and these pictures are unsurpassed in their atmospheric subtlety and range of effect. In subject matter, too, the *England and Wales* series provides a fascinating insight to the varied life and landscape of this country during a period of great social and technological change by one of the most acute social observers of his age. For many of the views in the series Turner relied on earlier material amassed in his voluminous sketchbooks, and upon his own remarkable memory. His travels throughout much of this period took him to Europe, and only in 1830, when revolution in France and Belgium prevented it, did he make a sketching tour of the Midlands specifically to gather material for *England and Wales.* But Wales did not feature on his itinerary, and all sixteen of the Welsh subjects that appear in the series were based upon his travels as a young man thirty years or more previously. His later treatment of these subjects makes a fascinating contrast with the paintings of his youth. Gone are the sombre tones and the carefully rendered architectural detail inherited from his days as a draughtsman. In their place are the hallmarks of the mature artist: grace of line, compositional structure and depth of meaning. But, above all, there is in these pictures an extraordinary intensity of colour and that exceptional rendering of the effects of light that was to become the principal and enduring characteristic of the artist in his later years.

NOTES

1. Herrmann 1975, 9
2. E. T. Cook and A. Wedderburn (eds), *The Works of John Ruskin* (London, 1903–12) Vol. 3, 616
3. Wilton 1984, 5
4. W. Thornbury, *The Life of J. M. W. Turner, R.A.* (London, 1862) Vol. II, 45–46
5. Wilton 1987, 19
6. R. & S. Redgrave, *A Century of Painters of the English School* (London, 1866) Vol. II, 83–84
7. W. Thornbury, *The Life of J. M. W. Turner, R.A.* (London, 1862) Vol. I, 27
8. Hamilton 1997, 20
9. Finberg 1961, 20
10. Wilton 1984, 5
11. The routes of this and Turner's subsequent Welsh tours are based upon Wilton 1984
12. C. Mackay, in *Burlington Magazine* 140 (1998), 383–86
13. British Library, Add. Ms. 46151 Ms K f.14, J. M. W. Turner, lecture manuscript
14. Finberg 1961, 50–51
15. Wilton 1984, 20–25
16. Shanes 2000, 14
17. Shanes, *Turner's Human Landscape*, 163ff
18. Quoted in Shanes, *Turner's Human Landscape*, 47
19. T. Green, *Extracts from the Diary of a Lover of Literature* (Ipswich, 1810) 3.VI.1799
20. Quoted in Wilton 1987, 36
21. Shanes, *Turner's Human Landscape*, 59ff
22. Ex inf. Andrew Wilton. See also Wilton 1984, 69
23. See Shanes, *Turner's Human Landscape*, 60, for a detailed interpretation of this view
24. Wilton 1979
25. Wilton 1979, 186
26. Quoted in Shanes, *Turner's England,* 13
27. See Shanes, *Turner's England*, 13–16, for further details on the project

SOUTH WALES TRAIL

1
LLANTHONY PRIORY

Set in the pleasant Vale of Ewias, the ruins of Llanthony Priory lie peacefully amid the rugged splendour of the Black Mountains. Some time around 1100, William, a knight in the service of Hugh de Lacy, stumbled upon a ruined chapel to St David here; thereafter he resolved to give up his arms and establish a hermitage. By 1118 Llanthony had become a priory for Augustinian canons and it was described by Gerald of Wales (d. 1223), towards the end of that century, as 'a religious site truly suited to the monastic life ... in a wilderness far removed from the bustle of mankind'. Enjoying the patronage of Henry I (1100–35) and Queen Matilda, the site grew rapidly, with as many as forty canons in its early years. The existing buildings date mainly from around 1175–1220, though the north transept underwent drastic alteration in the fourteenth century. The priory was suppressed in 1539, under Henry VIII (1509–47).

Its wild and mountainous setting made Llanthony an ideally attractive subject for Turner on his first tour in

Llanthony Abbey, *1794, pencil and watercolour: 327 x 424mm. Turner Bequest, Tate Gallery, London (BM: TB XXVII-R).*

Wales, in 1792. He made a pencil sketch of it on that tour, but several watercolours, based on this, were painted in 1794–95 as commissions for various patrons, of which the view shown here is one. With its composition based on the strong diagonal of the mountainside behind the abbey ruins, this is a powerful and atmospheric picture, which evokes all the expressive wildness and romantic 'Sublime' that was to be the hallmark of Turner's style later in the decade. Indeed it is clear, looking at the site today, that Turner deliberately decided to improve upon nature, for the view he painted is as impossible to obtain now, as it must have been then.

Llanthony Priory: set in the midst of the Black Mountains, from the north (Cadw).

The interior of Tintern Abbey, 1794, pencil and watercolour: 359 x 250mm. Turner Bequest, Tate Gallery, London (BM: TB XXIII-A).

2
TINTERN ABBEY

The gaunt remains of Tintern Abbey are still set seductively against the green, wooded valley of the River Wye, though not as isolated today as in the Middle Ages. Originally founded in 1131 for monks of the Cistercian order by the Norman lord of Chepstow, Walter de Clare (d. 1138), the great abbey church was rebuilt in the late thirteenth century with support from a later lord of Chepstow, Roger Bigod III (d. 1306). The abbey survived until 1536, at the dissolution of the monasteries under Henry VIII; Tintern was then the richest monastic house in Wales — wealth that is still reflected today in Tintern's great, soaring arches and elegant windows. The abbey church is the most dominant structure, still mainly intact and lacking only its roof, but there are extensive remains, too, of the other buildings which once served this thriving monastic community.

Turner visited Tintern on two of his tours through Wales, in 1792 and 1798, and painted the site a number of times. Interestingly, given the link between pictorial art and poetry referred to earlier (pp. 8–11), his two visits to the site coincided closely with those of the poet William Wordsworth (1770–1850). Wordsworth visited in 1793 and again in 1798 and it was during his second visit that he wrote his *Lines written a few miles above Tintern Abbey.* The two paintings included here are an untitled preparatory study of the interior of the crossing and presbytery with the east window and *The West Front of Tintern Abbey*, both of them based on pencil sketches made during the first visit, in 1792. These paintings were worked up in the winter after the tour and completed the following year, and they show the meticulous attention to architectural detail which was so characteristic of Turner's earlier work. But they are more than mere architectural studies, accomplished as they undoubtedly are in that respect; they are also splendidly scenic compositions, in which the artist's adoption of a low viewpoint ensures maximum dramatic effect from the soaring masonry, the closely clustered arches and the steep perspective.

Top right: *Tintern Abbey: the crossing and presbytery of the abbey church, from the west (Cadw).*

Bottom right: The West Front of Tintern Abbey, *about 1794, watercolour over pencil: 419 x 316mm. British Museum, London (1878-12-28-41).*

3
CHEPSTOW CASTLE

Chepstow Castle is situated on cliffs above the River Wye, where it guards one of the most important crossings between England and Wales. Although largely built in the thirteenth and fourteenth centuries, the original fortifications date back to the first decades of the Norman conquest of Wales. Occupied continuously until after the Civil War (1642–48), the castle underwent several periods of enlargement and improvement, both to its defences and its accommodation, and thus it illustrates to good effect the main stages in the development of military architecture throughout the Middle Ages. Despite all these later additions, its most striking feature is still the massive, rectangular stone keep built in the eleventh century.

Turner visited Chepstow on his very first tour of south Wales at the age of seventeen in the early summer of 1792. At that early stage in his career, the young artist's attentions were directed more towards the depiction of buildings than landscapes, and the ruins of Chepstow Castle standing proudly on its steep river cliff, guarding the river crossing, must have made an immediately attractive subject as he crossed over into Wales. His view shows the early timber-decked road bridge in the foreground, which was replaced by the present elegant iron structure in 1816. Inside the castle, Marten's Tower, to the left, still clearly retains its roof (though this has vanished long since), and the ruins of the early Norman great tower dominate the skyline above the cliff.

Chepstow Castle, *1793, watercolour: 203 x 297mm. The Courtauld Institute Gallery, London (1.74; Kitson 1).*

Chepstow Castle: situated on cliffs above the River Wye, from the east (Cadw).

Newport Castle, *1796, watercolour: 230 x 302mm. British Museum, London (1910-2-12-289).*

Newport Castle: the main facade from the east across the River Usk (Cadw).

4
NEWPORT CASTLE

Overlooking the muddy banks of the River Usk in the heart of the modern town, and now much beleaguered by modern roads and bridges, this once handsome nobleman's residence too often goes unnoticed. First fortified by the Normans before 1100, by the fourteenth century the lordship of Newport had passed through marriage to the earls of Stafford and the present castle was probably begun by Earl Hugh (d. 1386) between 1372 and 1386, though the side towards the town seems never to have been completed. Earl Hugh's grandson, Humphrey Stafford (d. 1460), set about a substantial remodelling of the castle between 1427 and 1457 to reflect his enhanced status, and much of the present structure is of this period. In later times the site had something of a chequered history and from 1820 to 1899 was converted into use as a brewery. Comprising one main range of buildings, fronting the river, there are the remains of the great hall, a grandiose central 'Presence Chamber', with a water-gate beneath, and a fine residential corner tower.

Turner visited Newport on his tour of 1795 and made a pencil drawing of the castle in his *South Wales* sketchbook. The watercolour reproduced here was based on that sketch, and was done the following year as a commission for a Mr Kershaw. The castle is viewed from across the river with its prominent central tower bathed in a shaft of gold sunlight and small boats clustered artfully around the water-gate at its base; to the left is the large residential tower and, to the right, part of the hall. Turner's view focuses attentively on the castle, which already shows signs of several later alterations; parts of the town, and the insubstantial-looking bridge, appear to the left of the composition.

5
EWENNY PRIORY

The Benedictine priory of Ewenny was founded in an existing church in 1141 by Maurice de Londres (d. 1149), Norman lord of Ogmore. Of all the monastic orders in Wales, that of the Benedictines was most closely associated with Norman colonization and their foundations were

Trancept of Ewenny Priory, Glamorganshire, *1796–97, pencil, watercolour and scraping-out: 400 x 559mm. National Museum of Wales (497a).*

Ewenny Priory: the crossing and south transept (Cadw).

rarely sited out of the shadow of the new castles and boroughs. Unusually, Ewenny occupies a rural location, but the fortress-like architecture of its priory church and the protective curtain wall which surrounds it are eloquent testimony of the political uncertainties which attended its early years. Although never a particularly wealthy house, conventual life continued here through to its suppression in 1539. The nave, like the rest of the church, dates from the early twelfth century and still serves as the parish church, but it is now physically separated from the eastern arm of the building, which is looked after by Cadw. Here the cavernous monastic choir, transept and chancel exhibit some of the finest Norman architecture to survive in Wales.

Turner visited Ewenny during his third tour in Wales, in 1795, and was clearly much moved by it. In contrast to his normal practice, this painting was uncommissioned and appears to have been done solely for the artist's own personal satisfaction. The reviewer of *St James's Chronicle*, writing in May 1797, considered it 'one of the grandest drawings he had ever seen, and equal to the best pictures of Rembrandt'; it is certainly the most important to result from the tour, and was exhibited at the Royal Academy in 1797. A comparison with the bare, undetailed pencil study on which the finished watercolour is based, done on site in the artist's sketchbook two years before, shows just how comprehensively Turner had come to understand architectural dynamics and how complete and retentive was his visual memory. The dark, enclosed and tomb-like interior of the church is dramatically illuminated by the ingenious introduction of two separate light sources, thus creating, in Andrew Wilton's words, 'a symphony of sonorous and shadowy colour'. The composition is provided with Turner's usual contemporary human interest by a man letting a pig through a door in the rood screen and a woman feeding the chickens which scratch about amongst the tombs.

6
CARREG CENNEN CASTLE

Standing at the summit of a mighty limestone crag that rises almost sheer some 300 feet (90m) above the River Cennen, Carreg Cennen Castle occupies a truly spectacular defensive position which demonstrates well all the adaptive skills of the medieval military architect. Though formerly a Welsh stronghold, belonging to the princes of Deheubarth, the building to be seen today was raised mainly in the late thirteenth century by Baron John Giffard (d. 1299), a loyal supporter of Edward I. Carreg Cennen was badly damaged by the forces of Owain Glyn Dŵr in the early 1400s, and finally demolished soon after 1462 by Yorkist supporters, during the Wars of the Roses (1455–85). One fascinating feature of the site is a narrow vaulted passage running down alongside the cliff face and leading to a natural cave beneath the rock; its purpose is uncertain, but it was probably to ensure security.

Carreg Cennen Castle: perched on a spectacular rocky crag, from the west at sunset (Cadw).

The view seen here was undertaken on Turner's fourth tour of Wales in 1798. This was his most extensive and ambitious Welsh tour, on which he planned to see the whole of the country, and his notes of places worth visiting included a large number of castles. Carreg Cennen's wild and spectacular location undoubtedly made it an ideal subject for an artist in search of the 'Romantic' and 'Picturesque'. This watercolour, from the west, takes up a double page in the sketchbook and, like other sketches in the volume, it has clearly been executed in some haste. The viewpoint selected is perhaps not the most dramatic that might have been chosen for this site, but, despite its sombre colours, it portrays to good effect the isolation and brooding dominance of the castle in its landscape.

Carreg Cennen Castle *in the* Dynevor Castle *sketchbook 1798 (ff.37v–38), pencil and watercolour: 135 x 220mm. Turner Bequest, Tate Gallery, London (BM: TB XL).*

Llandilo Bridge and Dinevor Castle, *1796, watercolour: 356 x 502mm. National Museum of Wales (498a).*

Dinefwr Castle: above the River Tywi from the west (Cadw).

7
DINEFWR CASTLE

Occupying a dramatic location, on the steep cliffs of the River Tywi, just on the outskirts of modern Llandeilo, Dinefwr Castle is of great symbolic importance in Welsh history as the ancestral seat of the rulers of Deheubarth, the ancient kingdom of south-west Wales. In the later twelfth century it was the principal stronghold of the powerful Rhys ap Gruffudd (d. 1197) — the Lord Rhys — who successfully restored much of the strength and influence of that ancient kingdom, but family feuds after his death led to the castle's decline and partial demolition. It was later captured and repaired by Edward I and survived as an English royal stronghold for the remainder of the Middle Ages. In later centuries, the castle was deliberately converted to a 'Romantic' ruin, and a summerhouse was built on the top of the keep. It now stands within the landscaped grounds of Newton House and can be reached on foot from within the park.

Turner would probably have known of the associations of the castle when he visited the site on his tours of 1795 and 1798. Although he made several colour studies in 1798, none survives from the 1795 tour, and yet the painting shown here — *Llandilo Bridge and Dinevor Castle* — is evidently based upon that tour, for it was completed in 1796. It is a powerful scene set at sunset; a broken stone bridge divides the composition, separating the ancient hilltop castle from the contemporary scene of countrywomen washing clothes in the river. The bridge at Llandeilo was apparently notoriously insecure at this period and was swept away regularly, the uprooted tree in the foreground of the picture being testimony to one such recent flood. Both castle and hill have been somewhat magnified and are shown considerably closer than in reality, but the sumptuous treatment of the light and the juxtaposition of past and present are typical of Turner's finest work.

Whilst this picture was undergoing conservation in 1993 an unexpected discovery was made which shed new light on Turner's experimentation with watercolour technique at this time. Bonded onto the back of the paper was another sheet painted with the same scene, though in a different technique and seemingly unfinished. At first this was thought to be a preparatory sketch which Turner had abandoned, but further investigation revealed that it was almost certainly a deliberate attempt to imitate in watercolour an effect which he had found possible with oil by superimposing layers of pigment. Here he seems to have tried to exploit the translucency of the watercolour paper and enrich the level of reflected light from the surface of the finished picture by placing additional painted work underneath the paper.

8
KIDWELLY CASTLE

In a commanding position above the River Gwendraeth, Kidwelly Castle's outer walls describe an almost complete semi-circle, following the curve

Kidwelly Castle: on the bank above the River Gwendraeth, from the south (Cadw).

Kidwelly Castle, South Wales, *1835, watercolour: 289 x 445mm. Harris Museum and Art Gallery, Preston.*

of the early stronghold raised soon after 1106 by the trusted confidant of Henry I, Bishop Roger of Salisbury (d. 1139). The present castle, with its concentric layout of one defensive wall within another, dates mainly from the late thirteenth and fourteenth centuries, when Payn (d. 1279) and Patrick de Chaworth (d. 1283), embarked upon its total reconstruction in stone. This began with the four-towered, rectangular inner ward and continued with the rebuilding of the great curving outer curtain wall. The main apartments of the inner ward are of early fourteenth-century date and adjoin a finely detailed chapel tower with prominent spur buttresses projecting towards the river. The massive twin-towered main gatehouse is mainly of fourteenth-century construction also, and is still the castle's most impressive feature.

Turner seems to have visited Kidwelly only once, on his tour of 1795, when he drew it from two differing aspects, although the site evidently left an impression on him, for he was to write to a fellow artist some years afterwards recommending it to his attention. The watercolour shown here was done long after that tour, in 1835, for the series of *Picturesque Views in England and Wales*. It is perhaps the best known of Turner's paintings of Welsh subjects and is generally acknowledged to be one of the finest examples of his output. In his mature years, Turner primarily conceived his work in terms of its colour, and the results are plain to see in this painting which is possessed of a radiant beauty, with the castle emerging through the swirling early-morning river mist; the contrast of the bright sunlight on the gatehouse and the pearly golds, pinks and soft bluey-purples on the remainder of the castle and the river estuary is quite breathtaking. The contemporary figures in the foreground — the young couple, horses and cart and the woman with her baby — add visual contrast and symbolic interest to the composition.

Llansteffan Castle: dominating the headland above the Tywi estuary, from the east (Cadw).

Llanstephan Castle by moonlight, with a kiln in the foreground, *1795, pencil and watercolour: 213 x 281mm. Turner Bequest, Tate Gallery, London (BM: TB XXVIII-D).*

9
LLANSTEFFAN CASTLE

The medieval castle of Llansteffan stands atop a high headland overlooking the Tywi estuary; its site, however, is one of much greater antiquity, having first been occupied by an Iron Age promontory fort in the sixth century B.C. The first definite reference to a medieval castle here is in 1146, when the site was taken by the Welsh, but from 1158 onwards the castle was mostly in English hands. The existing fortifications date mainly from the end of the twelfth and the thirteenth centuries; the inner ward, on the topmost part of the headland, is the earliest, with a small rectangular gatehouse and remains of a round tower. The lower ward was added in the latter part of the thirteenth century, its most prominent feature then, as now, being the great twin-towered gatehouse.

Turner visited Llansteffan during his journey into south-west Wales in 1795 and he painted this picture soon afterwards. The moonlit scene, with shimmering light reflected from the water, prefigures the same more developed effect in his first exhibited oil painting, *Fishermen at Sea*, of the following year (p. 6), and it was repeated in several subsequent pictures. Although the theme was evidently of some appeal, Turner never developed this particular view beyond its rather preliminary treatment here and, unfortunately, the watercolour has also been marred by some later staining on the paper. The kiln in the foreground adds considerably to the interest of the composition with the workers silhouetted in the bright firelight and smoke billowing from its top; it all makes a vivid and arresting contrast with the distant moonlit castle on its hilltop. Small-scale industrial processes of this kind were typical of south Wales at that time, for the area had yet to see the heavy industrialization that was to transform it in the early nineteenth century. What Turner recorded during those years was, for the most part, a secluded, rural land on which the influence of industrial processes was only just beginning to have an impact.

10
LAUGHARNE CASTLE

A Norman earth-and-timber castle was established at Laugharne probably before 1150, but this early fortification was rebuilt in stone during the thirteenth century by the de Brian family, who held the castle continuously until 1390. Almost two hundred years later Laugharne was granted to Sir John Perrot (d. 1592) by Queen Elizabeth I (1558–1603) in 1584. Perrot set about a systematic programme of enhancement and

Laugharne, or Talacharne Castle, Caermarthenshire, *about 1831, watercolour: 312 x 470mm. Columbus Museum of Art, Ohio: Bequest of Frederick W. Schumacher ([57]47.73).*

Laugharne Castle: the medieval castle at the mouth of the River Taf, from the south (Cadw).

modernization, making substantial changes to the gatehouse and adding a new hall block, but in 1592 he was convicted of treason and lost everything he owned. During the Civil War Laugharne was held by both sides, but was finally taken by the Parliamentarians in 1644 after a week-long siege and was then systematically demolished. Today the castle sits on its headland looking out to sea amidst a restored Victorian landscaped garden setting.

The painting seen here is one of Turner's series of *Picturesque Views in England and Wales*, and was completed around 1831, though the sketches on which the view is based were made on the tour of 1795. Although badly faded, it vividly depicts in the foreground the aftermath of a shipwreck, with atrocious seas and truly dramatic diagonal storm clouds, whilst a determined band of local salvage seekers brave the elements to carry off whatever they can. This is one of a number of instances where Turner depicts mankind pitted hopelessly against the elements, indeed wreck salvage featured several times, for it was, at the period, an accepted and economically important part of life for isolated coastal communities. To do so here he has, yet again, had to take some liberties with the topography: the castle has assumed somewhat heroic proportions and the river estuary has widened into a veritable ocean. In modern reality, the tide no longer comes right up to the castle as it probably did in Turner's day.

Pembroke Castle: across the Pembroke river, from the north (Pembroke Castle Trustees).

11
PEMBROKE CASTLE

Pembroke is tucked away on the farthest south-western peninsula of Wales — its Welsh name, Pen-fro, literally means 'land's end'. The area was colonized by Norman settlers very early on, and a castle was first founded on the site by Earl Roger of Montgomery around 1093. Soon after 1200 Pembroke passed to the great William Marshal (d. 1219) and, over the next thirty years, he set about building much of the stone castle that we see today. The defences enclose a very large area, divided into two separate wards, with round towers at the angles and a particularly impressive twin-towered gatehouse; but the most prominent and memorable feature is William Marshal's enormous free-standing round keep, its internal floors now missing, but still crowned by its massive stone dome and affording fine views from the top.

Turner seems only to have visited Pembroke in 1795; he painted the castle several times, but the first traceable view appeared some three years afterwards and others later still. The painting seen here is from *Picturesque Views in England and Wales* and dates from about 1830; its composition is based on two earlier views of 1801 and 1806, the first depicting a thunder storm approaching, the other clearing up after a storm. Andrew Wilton notes that Turner experimented several times with portrayals of a scene showing a castle beyond the sweep of a bay with fishermen in the foreground, but that Pembroke seems to have been his eventual choice. In this later view the sky and sea are less menacing than in the two earlier works, but the thunderstorm has grown rather more charged, with moisture seeming almost to hang in the air and William Marshal's somewhat elongated great tower rising up, spectre-like, in the background. The art critic of the *Observer* newspaper wrote of it in 1833 'the general effect is "terribly tropical", *hot, hot, all hot*'.

Pembroke Castle, Pembrokeshire, *about 1830, watercolour and scraping-out: 298 x 426mm. The Trustees of the Holburne Museum of Art, Bath.*

12
CAREW CASTLE

According to tradition, Carew was established by Gerald of Windsor, the constable of Pembroke Castle, at the beginning of the twelfth century, but of this castle nothing remains apart, perhaps, from earthworks. Most of the medieval parts of the existing castle were built around 1280 and 1310 for Sir Nicholas de Carew. To this period belong the outer curtain wall, the two hall ranges and the two splendid drum towers on the western side, with their prominent spur buttresses, so typical of the period around 1300. About 1480 the castle passed to Sir Rhys ap Thomas (d. 1525); between then and 1513 he made substantial changes to the structure and accommodation, but far more obvious today are the

Carew Castle: beside the Carew river, from the west (Pembrokeshire Coast National Park).

Carew Castle, Pembrokeshire, *about 1832, watercolour with body colour and scratching-out: 305 x 457mm. Manchester City Art Galleries (1917.99).*

additions of a later owner, Sir John Perrot who, between 1588 and 1592, was responsible for the splendid long range to the north, with its large windows and oriels projecting towards the river.

Turner visited Carew during his extensive tour through south and west Wales in 1795 and sketched it then, although no finished works of the castle are known from this time. The view shown here is from his series of *Picturesque Views in England and Wales* and dates from around 1832. The picture focuses on Sir Nicholas Carew's two great drum towers, but, once again, Turner has adjusted reality to suit the composition by altering the bend of the river to bring it nearer to the castle in the foreground, and heightening the vertical perspective of the castle to bring it closer. The structure of the picture is well conceived but it has been criticized for its rather 'hot' colour tone and it is not considered to be amongst his best work of the series.

13
ST DAVIDS BISHOP'S PALACE

The bishop's palace at St Davids nestles in a hollow beside the cathedral on the opposite bank of the River Alun. This ancient site is believed to be the *Vallis Rosina* — 'the valley of the little marsh' — where St David, patron saint of Wales, established a 'monastic' foundation in the sixth century. The surviving remains of the palace are largely the work of Bishop Henry de Gower between 1328 and 1347 and comprise three ranges of buildings around a large open courtyard. It was a grand and ornate building, as can still be seen today in the decorative arcaded parapet, chequered stonework and elaborately sculpted corbels which grace its wall-tops. St Davids was the largest and wealthiest diocese in medieval Wales; its bishops enjoyed the status of Marcher lords and the palace was clearly designed to reflect this.

St Davids Bishop's Palace: the porch to the great hall, from the north-east (Cadw).

The entrance to the Great Hall of the Bishop's Palace, St David's, *1795–96, pencil and watercolour: 411 x 257mm. Turner Bequest, Tate Gallery, London (BM: TB XXVIII-C).*

Turner visited St Davids on his tour of south Wales in 1795. On his way there he became fascinated with the indented and rocky coastline, of which he made several pencil studies, but the view seen here is the only one of the palace that survives. According to the artist's notes, he was actually commissioned to make a watercolour of the palace; this is presumably the beginning of his work on that, but it was never completed. It shows the grand entrance porch to the great hall; the peripheral areas are simply blocked in, but the archway itself and the other architectural details above are carefully drawn. Framed in the doorway, and bathed in golden sunlight, is a small group of cattle, though the detail here, as elsewhere, is unfinished.

14
CILGERRAN CASTLE

Perched on a rugged spur overlooking the steep gorge of the River Teifi, Cilgerran Castle is one of the most impressive defensive sites in Wales. A fortification was probably first established here by the Norman freebooter Gerald of Windsor around 1108, but the stone castle that can be seen today is the work begun by the powerful William Marshal the younger (d.1231), who wrested control of the area from Prince Llywelyn the Great (d.1240) in 1223. The principal features of the castle are the two massive drum towers, straddling the curtain wall, which bestow a stern and businesslike air to the defences on the landward side. However, it is from the river that the defensive qualities of the site are best appreciated — indeed Cilgerran's spectacular siting and 'Romantic' appeal made it a perennially popular destination for eighteenth- and nineteenth-century artists and tourists, who journeyed to the castle on boat trips up the river from Cardigan.

Turner took such a boat trip in 1798. Cilgerran greatly attracted him (as did a number of other castles poised on cliffs above rivers) and he painted it several times, portraying different effects of light and colour. The picture shown here is a fully worked-up watercolour in the *Hereford Court* sketchbook, which he took with him on that tour and in which there are also various other sketches of the site. A watercolour view and four oil paintings, based on these sketches, were completed the following year — a measure of Turner's fascination with this castle — and he was even to return to it once again, in 1828, for his series of *Picturesque Views in England and Wales.*

Cilgerran Castle: glimpsed above the River Teifi, from the south-east (Cadw).

Cilgerran Castle from the east *in the* Hereford Court *sketchbook, 1798, (f.100), watercolour: 229 x 332mm. Turner Bequest, Tate Gallery, London (BM: TB XXXVIII).*

The ruins of Valle Crucis Abbey, with Dinas Brân beyond, *1794–95, pencil and watercolour with some scraping-out: 460 x 375mm. Turner Bequest, Tate Gallery, London (BM: TB XXVIII-R).*

NORTH WALES TRAIL

1
VALLE CRUCIS ABBEY

The Cistercian abbey of Valle Crucis lies two miles outside the town of Llangollen at the foot of the Horseshoe Pass. Founded in 1201 by Madog ap Gruffudd Maelor (d. 1236), it was initially colonized by monks from the abbey of Strata Marcella. The site, in a remote and tranquil valley beside a plentiful supply of water, is typically Cistercian and its name means 'the Valley of the Cross' — from the nearby ninth-century Pillar of Eliseg. Construction work on the abbey began soon after its foundation, but there was major rebuilding after a disastrous fire in the mid-thirteenth century.

Valle Crucis Abbey: nestling below the Horseshoe Pass with Castell Dinas Brân above (Cadw).

Features of note for the modern visitor are the vaulted chapter house, which survives splendidly intact, the lofty monks' dormitory on the floor above it and the monastic fishpond, just to the north-east of the church.

The watercolour above is based on a study made during the tour of 1794, when Turner first visited north-east Wales. It is an ambitious and powerful painting; the sombre greens and browns of the dark, wooded foreground, where a young woman tends her pigs before the west front of the abbey church, are in sharp contrast with the sunlit mountainside behind and the distant ruins of Castell Dinas Brân, looming through the mist above. In its composition, as Andrew Wilton notes, the painting exhibits an almost chronological stratigraphy, in its lighting, as well as in the placing of the subjects: the ancient fortification at the top of the picture, the ecclesiastical remains in the valley and the view of contemporary life in the foreground. Turner was much later to repaint this scene, though very differently, in his series of *Picturesque Views in England and Wales* in 1826.

2
FLINT CASTLE

Flint was the first castle of King Edward I's initial military campaign in Wales of 1276–77. Surrounded by the waters of the Dee estuary, it was built to a four-square plan, but with the unusual feature that one of its round corner towers was larger than the others and isolated from the remainder of the castle, forming, in effect, a separate keep — though it seems likely that this was never completed to its full height. Flint Castle is perhaps best known for its role in events at the end of Richard II's reign (1377–99), when the king was captured here by Henry Bolingbroke, who became Henry IV (1399–1413) — a scene immortalized in Shakespeare's *Richard II*.

Turner visited Flint on all three of his tours through north Wales, in 1794, 1798 and 1799, but few works are known from these early visits. The picture here dates from 1835, and was done for the series of *Picturesque Views in*

Flint Castle: beside the mudflats of the Dee estuary, from the north-east at sunrise (Cadw).

England and Wales, though another similar view dates from the 1820s. The painting was acquired by John Ruskin, who later wrote of it: 'This is the loveliest piece of pure watercolour painting in my whole collection; nor do I know anything elsewhere that can compare, and little that can rival, the play of light on the sea surface and the infinite purity of colour in the ripples of it as they near the sand'. Certainly this view of the castle and estuary at sunrise is one of the finest in the series, demonstrating to the full Turner's technical and visual mastery. The careful rendering of detail, with fishing boats and shrimpers in the foreground, together with the purity of colour in the sky, the washed-out reflection of the sun on the water and the swirling early morning mist bestow on the painting an almost dreamlike quality which is especially memorable.

Flint Castle, North Wales, *1835, watercolour: 265 x 391mm.*
National Museum of Wales.

3
CONWY CASTLE

Built between 1283 and 1287 by Edward I, Conwy Castle and its associated circuit of town walls is now a World Heritage Site and one of the finest surviving examples of medieval military architecture anywhere in Europe. The castle, built on the west bank of the Conwy estuary, was the first to be established by Edward I during his second military campaign in Wales of 1282–83 and was virtually complete within only four and a half building seasons — an astonishing achievement, even by modern standards. Its massive curtain walls and eight cylindrical towers enclose two separately defended wards; the inner of these, distinguishable by its four turrets, contained apartments designed for the king and queen. Even today, despite the modern bridges which now abut it, the massed walls and towers of the castle present a strikingly powerful impression to travellers crossing the river estuary.

Conwy was on the itinerary of two of Turner's tours, in 1798 and 1799. He made numerous sketches on the site and completed several watercolours shortly afterwards. The view here is an oil painting, and was apparently commissioned by one of his previous patrons, William Leader, from a drawing in the *Hereford Court* sketchbook; it was probably completed in 1802–03, after Turner had returned from his first continental tour. The low viewpoint, menacing sky and the scattered flotsam on a brightly lit foreground all combine to emphasize the distant, brooding bulk of the castle on its rock jutting into the river estuary.

Conwy Castle: with the river estuary and transport crossings, from the south (Cadw).

Conway Castle, *1802–03, oil on canvas: 1035 x 1397mm. By kind permission of His Grace the Duke of Westminster, TD DL.*

Beaumaris Castle, Isle of Anglesea, *1835, watercolour and bodycolour with scraping-out: 295 x 420mm. Henry Huntington Museum, San Marino, California, U.S.A. (65.10).*

4
BEAUMARIS CASTLE

Beaumaris was the last and largest of all the castles built by Edward I during his conquest of Wales. In its planning, even if not in final execution, it was also the most impressive of them. Laid out on a flat, marshy site — its name comes from the Norman French *Beau Mareys* ('beautiful marsh') — this World Heritage Site is the ultimate concentric castle, its double ring of curtain walls disposed in near perfect symmetry to provide a sequence of mutually supportive defences quite without parallel. Construction began in 1295 and vast amounts of money and manpower were quickly lavished on the

Beaumaris Castle: set low on the coast with Snowdonia to the south (Cadw).

project, which progressed with astonishing speed. However, that initial investment was not maintained and construction work ground virtually to a halt within three years, leaving the inner towers, gatehouses and accommodation all incomplete. Still partially surrounded by its moat, which includes a dock for shipping, 'beautiful' is, even now, a fitting adjective with which to describe this castle, though its profile remains tantalizingly truncated.

Although Turner apparently visited Beaumaris in 1798, no sketches of it appear in any of his sketchbooks. The watercolour reproduced here comes from his series of *Picturesque Views in England and Wales*, and was painted as late as 1835. Perhaps not surprisingly, after such an interval of time, the topographical details of the foreground are totally incorrect, for there is no coastline in the position shown. Turner's usual depiction of local activity is introduced here with the anchored fishing boat and various groups of mussel gatherers on the shoreline. The bright touches of colour in the costumes of the little group in the foreground contrast with the delicately rendered evening light on the distant mountains beyond the Menai Strait.

5
CAERNARFON CASTLE

Caernarfon Castle is a World Heritage Site and unquestionably one of Europe's great medieval fortresses. Its majestic walls, angular towers and bands of coloured stone were all designed to impress as much as to defend, for they were modelled on the late Roman walls of Constantinople — one of the wonders of the ancient world. Begun by Edward I in 1283 during his

Caernarvon Castle, Wales, *about 1833, watercolour over traces of pencil: 278 x 418mm. British Museum, London (1958-7-12-439).*

Caernarfon Castle: reflected in the waters of the Seiont estuary, from the south-east (Cadw).

second campaign of conquest in north Wales, Caernarfon was designed to be both fortress and palace. As the principal administrative centre for the newly-formed shire counties of north Wales, and a fitting residence for the king's representative in the Principality, it was no coincidence that his son, the future Edward II (1307–27), was born at the castle early in 1284 and created prince of Wales in 1301. In the event, the castle never did serve that latter residential purpose; even so, more than seven hundred years on, its sheer size and defensive complexity still dominate and overawe visitors.

Turner visited Caernarfon on two consecutive tours in 1798 and 1799, as a result of which he produced a number of studies of the site (see inside front cover and p. 10). The watercolour shown here, completed around 1833, dates from long afterwards and is from his series of *Picturesque Views in England and Wales*; it has the gentler, more muted tones that characterize much of Turner's later work. The castle rises dreamlike out of the early evening mist, its looming bulk swathed in palest golds and lilacs; the earlier heat of the day is evoked by the group of girls bathing naked from a small boat in the foreground and some horses wallowing beyond. At the top of the picture, completing the composition, though impossibly close to the setting sun in reality, is a pale new moon.

Dolbadarn Castle: above Llyn Peris, surrounded by mountains and swathed with morning mist (Cadw).

6
DOLBADARN CASTLE

Perched amidst wild mountain scenery on a rocky outcrop between Llyn Padarn and Llyn Peris, Dolbadarn Castle occupies a spectacular and memorable position. It was built by Llywelyn the Great, prince of Gwynedd, probably around 1230, to command the entrance to the Llanberis Pass and its most notable feature is the great round stone keep, which still dominates its surroundings. According to tradition it was here that Llywelyn's grandson, Llywelyn the Last, imprisoned his brother, Owain Goch, for more than twenty years (p. 11).

Turner visited Dolbadarn on his fourth tour in 1798 and again the following year, when he completed a number of colour studies. The earlier of the two works reproduced in this booklet, the oil painting *Dolbadern Castle, North Wales* (p. 2) was the painting Turner offered as his Diploma work to the Royal Academy and it has already been described in some detail (p. 11). The other view reproduced here, showing a distant view of Dolbadarn is a watercolour of around 1832 from the series *Picturesque Views in England and Wales* and it was to be Turner's last British mountain subject. Entitled *Llanberris Lake and Snowdon, Caernarvonshire*, it is a wild and powerful scene, full of movement, in which the subtle interplay of light causes the mountains and the stormy sky almost to fuse together into one. The peak of Snowdon looms, Alpine-like, immediately above the carefully placed gap in the three lone trees at the right whilst from a rocky outcrop a mother and child — a device Turner uses several times in juxtaposition to ruins, for example at Kidwelly (p. 26) and at Flint (p. 39) — watch the two fishermen on the lake shore below. Far out on its rocky eminence above the lake, with the mountain slopes on both sides of the valley sweeping down to meet it, sits the solitary tower of Dolbadarn, bathed in a shaft of sunlight.

7
CRICCIETH CASTLE

Criccieth Castle stands in a commanding position on a high rocky promontory with spectacular views over Tremadog Bay at the base of the Lleyn Peninsula. Its most prominent feature is the twin-towered inner gatehouse, built by Llywelyn the Great, prince of Gwynedd, who established the castle in the 1230s. As the castle changed hands, so its defences were updated and enlarged: first by Llywelyn's grandson, Llywelyn the Last, and then, in turn, by Edward I and Edward II. Its end came in 1404, during the uprising under Owain Glyn Dŵr: deprived of sea-borne victuals, its English garrison was obliged to surrender and the castle was sacked and burned, never to rise again.

Turner seems to have visited Criccieth only once, on the tour of 1798, though no drawings of the site

Llanberris Lake and Snowdon, Caernarvonshire, *about 1832, watercolour and some bodycolour: 314 x 470mm. National Gallery of Scotland, Edinburgh (844).*

Criccieth Castle: on a high rocky promontory above the waters of Tremadog Bay, from the east (Cadw).

are known from that date. The watercolour shown here — *Crickieth Castle, North Wales* — is from the series of *Picturesque Views in England and Wales* and was painted late in the project in the summer of 1836. It illustrates a recurring theme in the series: wreck and ruin accompanied by man's vain attempt to salvage whatever he can; here a storm has left shipwrecked men on the beach, their salvage efforts being supervised by coastguard officers on horseback. The stormy waves still lash the shore, whilst the castle on its heightened rock looms majestically through the dark storm clouds. But this painting also illustrates another trait of the artist alluded to earlier (p. 11). As an erstwhile architectural draughtsman, Turner had always been conscious of form in buildings; the massive bulk of these castles in Wales gave him a new sense of their sculptural presence, and in attempting to capture this he would hastily sketch them from many different angles in order to gain a more complete understanding. This perception of the three-dimensionality of a castle led him, later on, to superimpose different orientations in a single view. He has done so here, for Criccieth Castle has been turned through 180 degrees upon its rock, as comparison with the photographer's view makes quite clear.

8
HARLECH CASTLE

Mainly completed between 1283 and 1289 for Edward I, this World Heritage Site confidently bestrides its rock some 200 feet (60m) above the coastal plain beneath. Its close-set concentric defences, massive inner gatehouse and the fortified stairway leading down to a landing stage at the foot of the rock all testify to the genius of its creator, King Edward I's chief military architect, Master James of St George. Harlech Castle had

Crickieth Castle, North Wales, *1836, watercolour: 290 x 425mm. British Museum, London (1958-7-12-440).*

something of a chequered history: in 1404 it was captured by Owain Glyn Dŵr who held it for nearly five years before it was retaken with siege and bombardment; it was again besieged in 1468 during the Wars of the Roses, and once more at the end of the Civil War in 1647, after which it was rendered untenable. Modern-day visitors will be rewarded with spectacular and panoramic views over Cardigan Bay, the mountains of Snowdonia and the Lleyn Peninsula.

The tour of 1798 provided Turner with several sketches of Harlech, some of which were worked up with colour. After it he was commissioned by the Hon. Edward Spencer Cowper to produce the oil painting seen opposite, based on a study in the *North Wales* sketchbook. Entitled *Harlech Castle, from Twgwyn ferry, summer's evening twilight*, Turner showed it at the Royal Academy accompanied by the following lines of verse from Book IV of Milton's *Paradise Lost*:

> *Now came still evening on, and twilight grey,*
> *Had in her sober livery all things clad.*
> *Hesperus that led*
> *The starry host rode brightest till the moon*
> *Rising in clouded majesty unveiled her peerless light.*

It is a splendid and atmospheric painting, wreathed in the browns and golds of evening light, the rigging of the ships silhouetted against the sky, and the castle imposing and distant upon its rock.

Harlech Castle: high up on a rock, looking out to sea, from the north-east (Cadw).